WHOLE IN THE BODY

Healing our way home
through the body's wisdom

By Sez Kristiansen

Bulk buy copies are available at a discounted rate. Contact Sez for more information.

hello@sezkristiansen.com
www.sezkristiansen.com
@sez.kristiansen

≈

Other books, kindle editions & audiobooks
by Sez Kristiansen:

Healing HER *(poetry for healing through the powers of the Divine Feminine)*

Story Medicine *(poetry & short story to heal every soul-sickness)*

The Daily Heal Journal *(guided prompt companion for emotional triggers)*

Inspired Mama *(non-fictional guide for mothers who want to create an intentional life)*

The Spoken Remedy *(podcast for guided meditations & healing poetry)*

≈

○

This book
is dedicated to
the body
who wishes
to return home
to its owner.

INTRODUCTION

ɘïɞ

The monarch butterfly has much to teach us about wholeness and what it means to embody an innate wisdom that we spend so much of our lives in search of.

This endangered species makes one of the greatest migratory journeys known on earth – and yet we know very little about how they accomplish such a task without a map or compass.

Every winter, tens of millions of monarch butterflies migrate from Canada to Mexico. They travel thousands of miles south to the same overwintering mountains as their ancestors did. The beauty and mystery of this species extend further to an even more incredible phenomenon: it takes up to five generations to complete one full cycle of migration.

On the way back from Mexico, monarchs produce offspring that carry the journey onwards for them. That means only their great-grandchildren return to their homelands. The ones that perish are the ones that make sure that the next generation carries the map and compass within the fragile folds of their bodies.

When the monarchs arrive back in Canada, something quite remarkable happens. The next offspring born from these homecomers are what is considered a *super generation.* That means they can live eight times longer and can travel back down to Mexico in just one lifespan. These super generations are also much stronger and more resilient than their forbearers.

The question that most people ask about this flutter-folk is how they transmit their map and the compass to their offspring, who have never traveled migration routes before, and who are born, sometimes thousands of miles away from home.

These second and third generations are born without knowledge, without guidance, and without the language we assume it would take to impart such wisdom. Somehow they *just know* how to return home. They just know to always keep the sun to their left and the moon to their right. They just know that milkweed is the only plant that can support their needs. They may read the wind, but the language required to interpret it already exists within them. They trust their individual part within a greater cycle, even if it means that they are not the ones to reach home - but are the bearers of a sacred torch that gets passed down to their young.

We too are fragile beings bearing the weight of a journey that we do not yet know what part we're playing.

We too long to return home. We hunger to return to the fullness of our bodies because they are what carries the fracture of our greater longing to be a part of a whole. Our bodies know the way. They *just know* what we need to heal our minds and hearts, and how to move through this life with a deep-seated trust in our intuition.

Our bodies have spent tens of thousands of years evolving under a western sun and an eastern moon, a northern ocean, and a southern fire. They have come to understand the ways of healing through smoke and story, through the wisdom of plants and through those who wrote remedies in stars, so that we could find our way home again. Our bodies remember, as did the bodies of all who came before us. This lifelong journey home to discover where we belong is a collective story we all share. It is our story of what it means to be human.

Disconnection is a divorce between our map and compass, our heart and mind – and this separation is now the most fatal disease we face in modern society.

But healing is where we begin to mend the void, those holes in the body, in order to remember our greater wholeness. And this process won't be a gaining but more a remembering of who we already are and what we already know. Because that is usually how disembodiment first occurs; that point in our past where we were made to believe that our wholeness was conditional and to be found outside of us.

We will go through many birth/death/and rebirths along the path towards holistic healing – many pieces of our pasts will have to fall away in order to make space for the new to carry our message of hope into the future.

But it's not what's left behind that completes our journey – it's what we offer tomorrow. It's the lessons we've learned from past struggles. It's the dreams we make sacred for our futures. It's the rewilding of our hearts and re-storying of our pain, so that we can invite a more liberating relationship into our lives. It's trusting that some parts of our lives are simply there to create the movement we need to keep going. It's the understanding that every part of us is welcome to exist here without shame, without judgment, and without it splintering us off from our wholeness.

If we begin to trust ourselves, in our *just knowings*, and our wilder ways, then we will begin to live each day with a little more attention and presence, and with a lot less impatience. We might even begin to recognize the necessity of loss, for it's only from its wake that new life is brought forth. And just as the monarchs return home, time and time again, so too must we remember that our own homecoming is a practice – one that we are ultimately made much stronger for.

This book of poetry and reflection is not only a reminder of our innate wholeness – it is a lifelong journey we all take to find our place of belonging in the very bones we inhabit.

To return to one's life is really to return to one's body. And we can only do this by first leaving what we have come to believe is true. We need to migrate when the wind carries its frosty kisses upon the northern current. We must learn to read this squall of longing that asks us to leave this place for more soul-enriching ones. We must trust that our bodies can tell the difference between the milkweed and the dogbane – or the right advice, the right partner, the right decision, the right career and differentiate them from their weaker substitutes. Because we cannot come home if we cannot trust. We cannot belong if we seek validation for our non-belongingness.

You *are* the greater whole, the absolute truth carried within the limitations of a perishable body. And no matter what your body looks like or what state it is in, *it* is not who you ultimately are.

You have so much untaught wisdom in you right now, and if you begin to trust in these mysterious *just knowings*, you will come to know the completeness of who you already are.

Together, we are a kaleidoscope of butterflies: each a whole piece, contributing to the entirety and beauty of another. Just as each limb, each freckle, each battle, each emotion, each loss, and victory makes up for the entirety and beauty of who you are.

May this book return you to your body, your home and the innate wisdom that resides within. And may you pass this torch of *knowing* onwards, so that it illuminates the way ahead for others.

poem / one

∞

The first story told
was the one
where you survived.

You did not perish
when you gave up,
when you got lost,
when you broke,
or wailed from the
depths of your loneliness.

You survived.

And so too shall
you wake up again
tomorrow with the
story of your bravery
tattooed upon your heart -
because only survivors get to
wear their courage this way.

poem / two

∞

Healing is not only for the
the strong and the saintly.

It is for all those who are willing
to move a mountain
one grass blade at a time.

poem / three

∞

○

Let your body love you.

poem / four

∞

Dis-abled,
dis-eased,
dis-embodied -
these words all come
from the name
of *Dis*, a Roman
underworld god
who was wealthy
beyond measure
because of his darkness.

We are therefor
made able,
made at ease,
made embodied
through the richness
of shadow and reflection.

And so, we become able,
not only by what we have,
but also,
and above all -
what we don't.

We become at ease,
not only by what we have,
but also,

and above all -
what we don't.

We become embodied
not only by what we have,
but also,
and above all -
what we don't.

Your *Dis* is a
what makes you
remarkably able,
just as your darkness
is what makes you
extraordinarily divine.

poem / five

∞

If you numb the body,
it will have to scream
before you can hear it.

So make time to listen,
to feel, to allow its
subtle voice to whisper
its way towards you.

And once you have
learned to speak *body* -
it will begin tell you everything.

poem / six

∞

Don't give up being kind
to yourself.

Because somewhere
on this body of yours,
there's a wound
with the exact shape
of your words.

poem / seven

∞

How rarely we
mention the body
as a gateway to belonging.

Its silence speaks volumes.

poem / eight

∞

°

You are always welcome in a body that is free to be itself.

p o e m / n i n e

∞

How deep runs her beauty
as she gathers more years.

How deep runs her beauty
as she weathers the storm.

How deep runs her beauty
as she buries her losses,
and how brave is her body
for still holding on.

p o e m / t e n

∞

The body
is only a prison
to those
who've forgotten
that pain
is a doorway.

p o e m / e l e v e n

∞

Nourish yourself
through the receptivity
of your wounds.

They are what makes you
most porous to magic.

p o e m / t w e l v e

∞

The body holds two pots within it,
one is glazed and the other isn't.

The glazed pot is heavy and reliable,
and can carry us through the hardships we
face in life, like it does water,
without spilling a drop.

But the unglazed pot is cleaved
and always light for it has an opening
that allows sorrows and fears and
good nourishments to be shared -
to flow outward from its fracture
with grace.

The unglazed pot, despite its imperfections,
nourishes the earth,
and waters the flowers with the contents
that seeps through its cracks,
touching every life force
it comes into contact with.

p o e m / t h i r t e e n

∞

○

The most empowering three words you can ever say to your body is:

This is normal.

poem / fourteen

∞

The difference between
a dot and a line –
is continuation.

So too is the
difference between
staying broken and
becoming healed.

Keep going.

poem / fifteen

∞

We spend
so much time
worrying about
how approachable
our bodies
that we rarely consider
how approachable we might be
to our bodies.

p o e m / s i x t e e n

∞

Your skin
defines the edges
of you in this world.
and yet the universe
seeps right through you.

p o e m / s e v e n t e e n

∞

You cannot be free if you keep hushing
that thunder in your belly.

You cannot speak if you keep apologizing
for that fire in your heart.

You cannot be truly connected if you keep locking
that door to your underworld.

You cannot allow the curves of your body to be
loved if you find them yourself, unlovable.

Because a whole body is an untamed one.

poem / eighteen

∞

What's greater than medicine?

A placebo.

Everything is tested against
the body's ability
to make you believe
in your wholeness.

p o e m / n i n e t e e n

∞

There isn't a body
in this world
that hasn't wanted to
pull itself away from life
and bury itself deep
beneath the earth, far away
from pain.

And in that soil
the body turns cold,
flesh is whispered away
by the passing winds,
and all that is left
are the bones
where no hurt can
meat itself upon.

And after the winters
have come and gone,
and come and gone…
and after the stones
and grass blades
have grown over and
all the way through
the body…
and after the rains
have drenched

and saturated,
and the sun has dried
and bleached…

Something will happen.

This body will
suddenly want to
remember what the
stars looked like
and what spring smells like,
and what touch feels like.

It will come like a calling
from beyond the horizon
and the body will long
to feel again.

And in listening to
that calling, the body will
begin to flesh itself out.

Every desire
will light a flame to live.

And by this fire,
you will be reborn.

p o e m / t w e n t y

∞

No body felt itself trusted
more than the one
that was let off
its leash.

poem / twenty-one

∞

There's nothing
more beautiful
than a body
full of surprises.

poem / twenty-two

∞

You have to be able to live
your questions before you
can answer them.

And once you have lived
them inside out, back to front
and even in your dreams,
you will come to see
that you are living
the very answers themselves.

poem / twenty-three

∞

○

Where in your body
do the wolves need to return to?

p o e m / t w e n t y – f o u r

∞

You do not need
to keep the secret
of how you survived
from yourself
or others.

poem / twenty-five

∞

Earth didn't win the battle
for the Body.

Moon did.

You are celestial -
and your bones are laced
with a billion stars
that fell for your beauty.

poem / twenty-six

∞

You may crave to be
by water's edge
or have your belly
press upon the ground
while you smell the wild earth…

You may have to take
long walks across open fields
or stand on the cliff's crest
as you lean against the current…

You may have to pour yourself
into the canyon just to empty the
sadness or fill the lake with the shape
of your body in order to feel whole…

You may have to pull things
up from the soil or plant things
deep, deep down into it.
You may have to have your nails
thick with dirt in order to
cleanse your soul…

You may have to spend
more time with your body
being held by the slow-moving earth.
You may have to knead pastry dough,

or mend frayed hems or dip
elderberry flowers in your water.
You may need to smoke your skin
like haddock or sweat your prayers
like sins…

You may need to find a place
where only you know…

You may feel like you will perish
if you don't strip yourself of clothes
and run out into the storm.
You may need to relocate your
entire life just to watch the moon
from a more lonely sky.
You may need more tears just
to dip your paintbrush in.

You may need to do
many a wild act
in order to remember yourself.

p o e m / t w e n t y - s e v e n

∞

We do not need to be a biologist
to know our bodies.

All we need to know is
how to listen to them.

p o e m / t w e n t y - e i g h t

∞

Trust has a home
in the body -
and it's clearly
not in the mind.

poem / twenty-nine

∞

Fatigue is a body
who is always in search
for what it believes it's missing.

Aliveness is a body
creating what it needs
with what it already has.

poem / thirty

∞

Cry your body through.
Cry it inside out.
Wring it of all its sorrows.
Air it of its long years.
Pin it by wooden pegs
on the hanging line
and leave it out
in the sun to dry…

So something new can be worn.

poem / thirty-one

∞

Notice how your body
occupies this room.
Is it afraid to take up
too much space,
or is it filling it up
unashamedly?

Is it in pain and pinched
from the shoulders inward,
or does the spine wear your body
like a sail at full mast?

Is it subtly protecting itself
from an unknown threat,
never fully relaxed,
or is it buttered dough,
ready for life's shapings?

Your body does not simply
occupy this room,
it converses with it.
It holds stories from your past
within its cells and acts
as a living testament for
every event you have ever
been witness or participant to.

It's speaking now
as you read this book,
and like a child who has learned
to mimic its parent's language,
so too does your body speak
with the same voice
you have disciplined it with.

How you speak to your body
either feeds or severs it
from its intuitive power.

It's a choice which tool
you use to create your body with
but one thing is unequivocal;
the body is a humble
and loyal companion.

poem / thirty-two

∞

○

One of the hardest questions we can ever ask ourselves is, *what am I having to do in order to survive?*

poem / thirty-three

∞

How much the body is born with,
and how much it can be
whatever it wants to be.

That is the balance
we are all trying to find -
between the gifts of our history
and the intentions we have
to create our own destiny.

poem / thirty-four

∞

There may come time
in your life,
when living outside of
your body is so painful
that all you want to do
is find a hole in your skin -
just so you can crawl back into it.

And what you will realize is that
it isn't a hole you are seeking,
but a door -
and its welcome mat
is your addiction,
your habit, your pain…
and all you've been doing
these past few years
is knocking on that door,
only to run away again.

But every time you feel down
you will remember that
you are being invited in.

And every time you feel lost
you will remember that
you are being welcomed home.

And all you have to do
is cross the threshold.

All you have to do
is stay with the hurt
for just a moment -
because you'll see that
it's the running away
that breaks you -
not the opening of that door.

p o e m / t h i r t y - f i v e

∞

You cannot see
the beauty in the world
and in others
without that beauty already
existing within you.

Even on the hard days -
especially on the hard days -
find one thing to love
outside of yourself
and allow it to remind you
of what already exists within.

poem / thirty-six

∞

○

The primary purpose of the body is not to attract others.

p o e m / t h i r t y - s e v e n

∞

If you want
to live more
in the world,
live more in the body.

If you want
to live more
connected to spirit,
live more connected to
the body.

If you want
to live more
in love with another,
live more in love with
the body.

And if you want
to be more connected
to the body,
rest.

poem / thirty-eight

∞

There is no
such thing
as diversity –

For diversity
to occur,
you need an
individual
and then
separation.

You are not diverse
you are WHOLE.

poem / thirty-nine

∞

There is no word
to fully describe the
color of a woman.

She is each a
painting
of Love.

She is
the color
of amber -
with milkweed lips
and lemongrass veins.

She is taupe -
with creases of
cherry blossom
and powdered
eggshell earlobes.

She is ebony -
with linen colored heels
and oyster lashes.

She is porcelain -
with whispers of lilac
and heather on the small of her back.

She is pistachio -
with strokes of
cedar and cinnamon
in her hair.

She is violet
and midnight -
with dove colored palms
and pebble folds.

How to classify a woman
if not to use every shade
on a painter's palette.

She is anything but one color.

She is a prism,
a palette,
a masterpiece.

poem / forty

∞

The body seeks water
because it seeks ease.

The body seeks fire
because it seeks company.

The body seeks air
because it seeks life.

The body seeks earth
because it seeks
to become its apprentice.

poem / forty-one

∞

If you believe you are broken
then you will find a thousand ways
to validate that fracture.

If you believe you are whole
then you will find a thousand ways
to validate that completeness.

poem / forty-two

∞

You may not always
know where you are
but the trees know,
the raven knows,
the sky knows,
the ferns know…

Being lost is
one sided –
so just remember
that you are always
where you need to be.

poem / forty-three

∞

It's our unlived lives
that hurt our loved ones
most.

So pull the life
you are longing to live
out into the open.

And let your kin
see what it's like
to work for
what you ache for.

poem / forty-four

∞

The most radical acts
of self-love
come to us in those
small moments of
self-acceptance…

A body finding comfort
in discomfort.
A body finding ease
in dis-ease.
A body finding courage
to face what's passed.
A body deciding to hold on
to hope, despite it all.
A body that chooses the
vulnerability instead of
protecting itself.

These are the ways
we become the owners
of our lives,
the keepers of our hearts
and the stewards
of our bodies.

poem / forty-five

∞

Often,
we have to
give up a habit
to save a lung,
a kidney,
a heart…

But more often,
we have to give up
a belief
to save an entire life.

poem / forty-six

∞

◦

We spend our lives trying to escape the one thing
that can heal us.

The Body

poem / forty-seven

∞

There's nothing more lethal
than a repeated word.

There's nothing more remedial
that a repeated word.

You get to choose.

poem / forty-eight

∞

Your culture will steal you
away every day.

It's your job to steal yourself
back every night.

So dream of
untamed and wilder
places with the hope
that one morning
you will wake up
with your
fur still on.

poem / forty-nine

∞

○

Be where the body is.
There is nowhere else that this pain can be healed.
There is nowhere else that this life can be lived.
There is nowhere else that this joy can unfold.

poem / fifty

∞

Our un-mothered mothers knew
something dangerous and
poisonous about this world.

That if we played with the untamed
and ate the wild,
something would begin
to work its way inside of us.

And if we ate too much,
we would no longer
fit into the suits
we had been given,
nor the jobs and homes,
nor the thoughts
and unforgiving plans
we had carved ourselves into.

Our hair would grow long
and disorderly.
Our shoulders would
fold back to expose
our vulnerable hearts.
Our blood would pump
faster under our thicker skin
and our bones would be
toughened like steel.

We would become
'unmanageable'.

A wild light would
flicker through our eyes,
and our words
would begin to sound
so strange;
profound and deep,
laced with poetry and dream,
and all wonders
of impracticality.

And the more we would eat of it,
the more we would come alive.

Our un-mothered mothers
knew of this wild
because they too, had tasted it,
but feared too much
the power it would unleash
inside of them,
and so they made warnings
to replace their losses -
secretly longing to feel
their wild hips
dance in the moonlight again
or commune with
the midnight lake as it
coveted itself in a cloak of stars.

But you still have a chance
to heed this warning
and go deep into the wild,
and eat what you find there.

Don't fear the power,
but use it to remove the venom
that already exists in this body
that makes you think
you need to be tamed
in order to be whole.

poem / fifty-one

∞

You are not this story
nor its author.

You are the light
that that shines
upon this page
so that life
can be read.

poem / fifty-two

∞

°

The problem doesn't lie in the body -
it lies in what *you* think of it.

poem / fifty-three

∞

Just as the honey in the jar
cannot see its own label,
so too can your body
not see what it is –
you have to tell it
everyday, about its
beauty, its gifts, its strengths,
its blessings, and its capabilities…

That way,
it will not only
know what it is -
but it will be delicious
to live in.

p o e m / f i f t y - f o u r

∞

Lose yourself
to the best of you.

To the love, to the slow -
to the rest, the hope,
and mendings of you...

And then evolve from that space.

Because if you have lose
your wholeness
in order to please a few -
you will forever stay
fish-tailed and web-footed.

And if your attention is being
farmed for the hunger
of others,
you will never taste the
full bellied wild.

Let the sediment of distraction
and should-do's
fall heavy to the bottom,
allowing stillness and light,
and fearlessness to arise.

For all can be healed,
grown,
created,
loved,
forgiven
through a body
that is fully
at rest
within itself.

poem / fifty-five

∞

The times we give up
on our bodies
happen to be when
we need them
most.

To heal is to know
when we are needed -
and then to have the courage
to stay with it.

poem / fifty-six

∞

Give *all* of you
a home.
Not just the parts
that others find
value in.

Let all the pieces of you
call your body Mother, and let
them find Love within her bones.

Let the messy parts of you know
they are loved without
the want of order.

Let the animal parts of you know
they are loved without
the want of taming.

For it's the want that hurts.
It is the need for the innocent
to be different that orphans them
from the very place of their belonging.

poem / fifty-seven

∞

For the journeys you
will have to face
throughout
your life,
you will be asked
but one question:

"Am I willing to
offer my body
to the cause,
and not just my mind?"

poem / fifty-eight

∞

○

All habits start in the mind -
not the body.

p o e m / f i f t y - n i n e

∞

Dreams are houses
we wish to inhabit.

So make sure
yours is cleaned
and tidied -
and that it
has rooms
and spaces
for others.

For a dream
built only for you
will be a lonely abode
and no amount of
wood you put in
the hearth will
make it warm.

And no amount
of windows will
give it light, nor
the quality of
materials ensure
its longevity.

Dreams were meant

to be shared with
those you love,
for it is their presence
that truly makes it a home.

poem / sixty

∞

Embodiment is messy.

It doesn't come as tailored
glove, ready for the hand.

It comes as fabric.
And scissors.
And pins.
And without measurements.

It comes as time
and failure. As rejection
and self-doubt.

It comes as a pattern-less promise.

It comes as a lifelong process,
of clipping and sewing as you grow.

It comes as raw material that
only *you* know what to do with.

But when you do fit yourself,
you will never want to try
and squeeze yourself
into anyone else.

p o e m / s i x t y - o n e

∞

What does it feel like
to not hold a body -
but a story?

A living transcript and record
of life as it lightly presses
upon your skin?

What is it like to live
in a book and not a body?

To wander the pages that mark
your years, your heart dog-eared
with events you wish to later revisit?

What is it like to be a storyteller
and not a character in your own life?

How would you write your tomorrows
and all the days after it?

p o e m / s i x t y - t w o

∞

○

The story you were born into
can be the story
you were rebirthed from.

poem / sixty-three
∞

Take a pen,
and on every wound,
ache or loss
you have on your body -
write the word,
Love.

Soon, you will realize
that you are
full of it.

poem / sixty-four

∞

For when you feel like
you can't possibly be healing…

Just imagine
for a moment
that every hurt ,
every rage,
every bruise,
every heartbreak,
every scrape,
every tear,
every loss,
every disease,
every cut,
you ever received
was still held by your body…

You *are* healing – as you have done
and will continue to do.

Trust in your body's wisdom
and its ability to do unseen work.

poem / sixty-five

∞

You can only progress
up to a point when
all desire for progress
must be abandoned
in order to make
further progress
possible.

poem / sixty-six

∞

If you dig down
and try to find
the origins
of your hurt,
you may only
find the bones
of all those
who went before.

Sometimes
slowly, intentionally
feeling your way ahead
is better than excavating
the past because some hurt
is not yours to hold -
but the residue
of a thousand lives
lived before yours.

poem / sixty-seven

∞

The most
sacred relationship
you have
is the one
between
your brokenness
and Love.

poem / sixty-eight

∞

Just as you can learn
something,
you can remember
something else
that's never been taught.

poem / sixty-nine

∞

Unmarked bodies
are bodies praised
as beautiful
by our culture.

But if you have lived -
you have scars.

Don't praise the lifeless.

Praise what has had
the audacity to live.

poem / seventy

∞

○

Instead of asking yourself why you couldn't just
be normal – ask yourself what is stopping you
from embodying your extraordinary.

poem / seventy-one

∞

Wanting the spiritual
without the body
is like wanting to fly
without the plane –
because there cannot be divinity
without the body,
just as wholeness cannot exist
without its container.

poem / seventy-two
∞

We cannot demand the body
to stop failing us,
but apologize for not listening
to it with more tenderness.

poem / seventy-three

∞

Wild women
allow thunder
to echo through them.

Wild men
learn to count
their Mississippi's.

poem / seventy-four

∞

There are few
and simple things
to remember on
the journey ahead:

Heaven is within,
you are always loved,
and no one holds the key
to your joy but you.

poem / seventy-five

∞

○

You don't need a different body.
You only need to have a different conversation
with it.

poem / seventy-six

∞

You and the person
next to you -
not matter what
they look like
or where they
are from -
share 99.95%
of the same DNA.

Say hi -
you're not that
different after all.

poem / seventy-seven

∞

Memory is a story that
gets integrated by the body.

But trauma does not.

Trauma is not remembered,
or re-storied.
Trauma is only ever
relived.

It's normal to distort memories –
to allow them to
change shape
as you grow.

But the trauma story
doesn't change over time.

It stands like a winter tree
on a summer's eve –
immortalized by fear.

To change a memory
is to heal
because our bodies
can only tell the stories
we choose to remember.

poem / seventy-eight

∞

○

To be free *in* the body,
you must first be free *of* the body.

p o e m / s e v e n t y - n i n e

∞

You didn't come here to
be protected.

You came here to love -
and be loved.

You came here to be devoured
because of your delicious heart.

And if this life makes you bitter –
which it will try –
you must find your way to
the nearest ocean
and fold your sweet-self
into its salty tide.

That way, you will preserve
your goodness.

That way, you will be able
to always offer yourself
without the fear of turning sour.

poem / eighty

∞

○

Age has a way of making the distance between you
and your body intolerable.

p o e m / e i g h t y - o n e

∞

The weight of losses
from a lifetime ago
still ripple against your body,
for you are the shore
to which an ocean of hurt
still breaks itself upon.

So feel the ache of arrows that
have never struck your skin -
but do not tend to them
as if it were *your* life in danger.

For your life is your own -
and the past is
but a phantom limb.

poem / eighty-two

∞

For the Elders you never had,
the fires you never sat by,
the tents you never entered,
the hands that never
held and healed you…

Your body remembers,
your blood remembers
because your emotions
were built in sync with a land
that was tended to,
by that which still
courses through you.

Atom-deep wisdom – it's all here
and ready to be drawn upon
in times of despair.

Because you, dear one,
are drawn upon -
by a cosmos who longed
to speak,
by a land who longed
to be witnessed,
by a moon who longed
for companionship,
and by the stars who wanted

to know what it was like to dance
upon the earth.

poem / eighty-three

∞

°

Wounds are quiet places.

p o e m / e i g h t y - f o u r

∞

Trust your body.
Every cell is on your side,
which means you have
hundreds of billions of allies.

poem / eighty-five

∞

Dear body,
this world is a beautiful place
and the smaller you feel in it,
the more you will remember
how fragile you are.

Place yourself in the listening area
of thunderstorms
or by the shore of raging wave.
Sit still among the
neon yellow rapeseed harvest
or by the stretching body of
sleeping lake.
By the foothills of mountains
unmoved by men
or on the lonely sand dunes
before sunrise…

You may forget your place
amongst people
but you will always remember
yourself again in the wild.

poem / eighty-six

∞

○

There are very few truths in this life.
And all that separates us is the journey we take to
discover them.

p o e m / e i g h t y - s e v e n

∞

Hold the grieving body
like an autumn tree.

Let it fall apart.

Cast its leaves
and seeds
upon the ground
and let its branches
hang bare.

Allow the cold
of winter's breath
to cut it
of its last green.

And when this body
has nothing left to offer,
begin to mourn.

For as grief is in the losing
so is rebirth in the mourning.

Spring will come
to the body once more
because all life is held
within its roots –

not in what can be seen
above the ground.

poem / eighty-eight

∞

It's ok to stop
defending yourself...

You're safe
in this body.

The past
doesn't live
here anymore.

poem / eighty-nine

∞

More heart. More feeling your way through. More acceptance. More openness. More light. More slow. More generosity. More love. More water. More fearlessness. More inclusivity. More care. More nature. More nourishing. More time. More surrender. More presence. More fun. More fierce. More no. More gratitude. More empowerment. More voice. More boundaries. More meaningful. More more. More deep. More dreaming. More intuitive. More trust. More here. More movement. More unconditional. More magic…

And if you cannot possibly fit *more* in…
then do only one thing *less*.

Less doubt in the deserving of more-ness.

poem / ninety

∞

○

You are whole not despite of your fracture but
because of it.

poem / ninety-one

∞

There's no
straighter way
back to the body
like touch,
music,
and movement.

Use it
like anchors -
like soft hands
pulling you back
into be-ing.

p o e m / n i n e t y - t w o

∞

What story would you like
to free from the body?

As if you could snip the fine thread
that has tied it to your breast like a button.

As if you could unweave it from your hips.

As if you could fluff it off your shoulder
or hit a flat spoon against it
and free its particles into sunlight.

What story has allowed moss to
grow over it?

As if you could uproot the tree
and turn it around so that
the darkness could stop growing
against the cold north.

What story no longer lives here?

As if you would redirect its mail
to a forwarding address
somewhere deep into the
soundless forest where all
old stories go to die.

Who would you be
without it
and what could be
written in its place?

poem / ninety-three

∞

For all the times
I wanted to
leave this life –
my body has
always
made me stay…

And for that
I am deeply thankful
that it didn't
always listen to me.

poem / ninety-four

∞

What if
you are exactly
where you need to be?

What if
you have everything
you need inside of you?

What if
it's just a matter
of patience and trust?

poem / ninety-five

∞

When did the
story of *desire*
become so tainted?

Desire from your body
for another body,
for goodness,
for more,
for better,
for different –
is natural.

It is only when desire
is sought after
for the sake of possession
that we suffer.

Desire is evolution,
and so it is fundamental
to the story of your life.

Change your relationship
with desire if needs be
but not the longing itself.

For we are all brought forth
from the seed of that ache.

poem / ninety-six

∞

And in the end,
is it not the constant
seeking for healing that
keeps us broken?

And to embody
the most sacred of truths
would be to say,

"I am healed.
I'm just taking time
to remind myself of it
everyday."

THE END

ɘïɞ

Thank you for reading this book. Not because you needed to learn something new about yourself, but because, like all of us, you may have needed a reminder of who you already are. That is both the fear and freedom of empowerment; that we are what we've been seeking all along.

I would love to know more about you and your journey back to embodying your wholeness, so please always feel free to connect with me:

www.sezkristiansen.com
hello@sezkristiansen.com
@sez.kristiansen

Together, we are a kaleidoscope of butterflies and your words map the way for others. For self-published authors like myself, writing a book that you want to share with another soul is the highest honor of achievement, so if this book resonated with you, please consider leaving a review on **Goodreads** or **Amazon**. Or better yet, pass this book on to a friend and offer it new life.

From my body to yours,
Sez

NOTES

When do I feel most embodied?

What part of my life do I tend to tame for the sake of others?

What makes me feel alive, wild and free? And what do I fear will happen if I embrace it more?

Where do I seek a sense of belonging from?

When did I last make an intuitive decision and how did it work out?

Printed in Great Britain
by Amazon

17963243R00071